Questions and Answers
OCEANS

Questions and Answers

OCEANS

Camilla de la Bedoyere
Anna Claybourne

Miles
Kelly

First published in 2014 by Miles Kelly Publishing Ltd
Harding's Barn, Bardfield End Green, Thaxted, Essex, CM6 3PX, UK

2 4 6 8 10 9 7 5 3 1

Publishing Director Belinda Gallagher
Creative Director Jo Cowan
Editors Claire Philip, Chlöe Schroeter
Designers Kayleigh Allen, Michelle Cannatella,
Andrew Crowson, Sally Lace, Joe Jones, Redmoor Design
Cover Designer Rob Hale
Production Manager Elizabeth Collins
Reprographics Stephan Davis, Jennifer Hunt, Thom Allaway

ISBN 978-1-78209-472-2

Printed in China

British Library Cataloguing-in-Publication Data
A catalogue record for this book is available from the British Library

ACKNOWLEDGEMENTS
The publishers would like to thank the following for the use of their photographs:
Cover Ernie Janes/Nature Picture Library
Dreamstime.com 59 Johnandersonphoto; 65 Goodolga; 67 Naluphoto
Fotolia.com 48 SLDigi; 50 Desertdiver; 55 cbpix
iStockphoto.com 71 Boris Tarasov
Rex Features 52 c.W. Disney/Everett
Shutterstock.com com 28 RoxyFer; 31 Photodynamic; 32 Specta; 33 javarman; 38 Glenn Price;
40 Jay Hood; 46 Niar; 53 bernd.neeser; 60 Levent Konuk; 62 A Cotton Photo; 69 tubuceo

All other photographs are from:
digitalSTOCK, digitalvision, Image State, John Foxx, PhotoAlto,
PhotoDisc, PhotoEssentials, PhotoPro, Stockbyte

All artworks from the Miles Kelly Artwork Bank

Every effort has been made to acknowledge the source and copyright holder of each picture.
Miles Kelly Publishing apologizes for any unintentional errors or omissions.

Made with paper from a sustainable forest
www.mileskelly.net   info@mileskelly.net

Contents

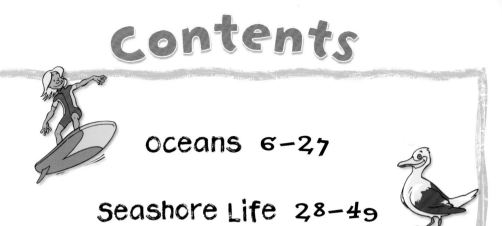

Is there only one big ocean?

It seems that way. All the oceans flow into each other, but we know them as four different oceans — the Pacific, Atlantic, Indian and Arctic. The land we live on, the continents, rises out of the oceans. More than two-thirds of the Earth's rocky surface is covered by oceans.

① ② ③ ④ ⑤

Key
① Arctic Ocean
② Atlantic Ocean
③ Pacific Ocean
④ Indian Ocean
⑤ Southern Ocean

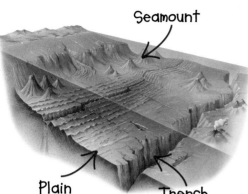

Seamount

Plain

Trench

Are there mountains under the sea?

Yes there are. The land beneath the sea is covered by mountains, flat areas called plains and deep valleys called trenches. There are also huge underwater volcanoes called seamounts.

Salty or fresh!

Almost all of the world's water is in the oceans. Only a tiny amount is in freshwater lakes and rivers.

Were do islands come from?

Islands are 'born' beneath the sea. If an underwater volcano erupts, it throws out hot, sticky lava. This cools and hardens in the water. Layers of lava build up and up, until a new island peeps above the waves.

Look

Look at the world map to find where you live. Which ocean is nearest to you?

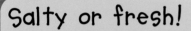

Do seashells have feet?

Tiny animals called limpets live inside some seashells. They stick to rocks at the shoreline where they eat slimy, green plants called algae. When the tide is out, limpets stick to the rocks like glue, with a strong muscular foot. They only move when the tide crashes in.

Limpets

Can starfish grow arms?

Yes they can. Starfish may have as many as 40 arms, called rays. If a hungry crab grabs hold of one, the starfish abandons its arm, and uses the others to make its getaway. It then begins to grow a new arm.

Anemone

Starfish

Fighting fit!

Anemones are a kind of sea-living plant. Some anemones fight over their feeding grounds. Beadlet anemones shoot sharp, tiny hooks at each other until the weakest one gives in.

When is a sponge like an animal?

Sponges are animals! They are very simple creatures that filter food from sea water. The natural sponge that you use in the bath is a long-dead dried-out sponge!

Crab

Sponge

Find

When you next visit a beach, try to find a rockpool. Write a list of what you see.

9

Are there schools in the sea?

Some fish live in big groups called schools. This may protect them from hungry hunters. There are thousands of different types of fish in the sea. Most are covered in shiny scales and use fins and tails to swim. Fish have gills that take in oxygen from the water so that they can breathe.

Read

What is a big group of fish called? Read this page to find out.

Which fish looks like an oar?

The oarfish does – and it can grow to be as long as four canoes! It is the longest bony fish and is found in all the world's oceans. Oarfish have a bright red fin along the length of their back. They swim upright through the water.

Oarfish

Flying high!

Flying fish cannot really fly. Fish can't survive out of water, but flying fish sometimes leap above the waves when they are swimming at high speed. They use their long fins to glide through the air for as long as 30 seconds.

Do fish like to sunbathe?

Sunfish like sunbathing. Ocean sunfish are huge fish that can weigh as much as one tonne – as heavy as a small car! They like to swim at the surface of the water, as if they're sunbathing.

School of fish

What is the scariest shark?

Great whites are the scariest sharks.
These huge fish speed through the
water at 30 kilometres an
hour. Unlike most fish, the
great white shark has warm blood. This allows
its muscles to work well but it also means that
it needs to eat lots of meat. Great white
sharks are fierce hunters. They will
attack and eat almost anything, but
prefer to feed on seals.

Great white shark

Draw
Using felt-tip
pens, draw your
own underwater
picture. Include a
great white shark.

Do some sharks use hammers?

Not really! Hammerhead sharks have hammer-shaped heads to search for food. With a nostril and an eye on each end of the 'hammer', they swing their heads from side to side, looking for a meal.

Hammerhead shark

Yum yum!

Most sharks are meat eaters. Herring are a favourite food for sand tiger and thresher sharks, while a hungry tiger shark will gobble up just about anything!

When is a shark like a pup?

When it's a baby. Young sharks are called pups. Some grow inside their mother's body. Others hatch from eggs straight into the sea.

Who builds walls beneath the sea?

Tiny animals build underwater walls.
These walls are made of coral,
the leftover skeletons of tiny sea
animals called polyps. Over millions
of years, enough skeletons pile up to
form walls. These make a coral reef.
All kinds of creatures live around a reef.

Parrot fish

Seahorse

Look
Do you know
where the Great
Barrier Reef is?
Look in an atlas
to find out.

Clownfish

How do fish keep clean?

Cleaner wrasse are little fish that help other fish to keep clean! Larger fish, such as groupers and moray eels, visit the cleaner wrasse, which nibbles all the bugs and bits of dirt off the bigger fishes' bodies – what a feast!

Super reef

You can see the Great Barrier Reef from space! At over 2000 kilometres long, it is the largest thing ever built by living creatures.

Coral reef

Lionfish

Cleaner wrasse fish

When is a fish like a clown?

When it's a clownfish. These fish are brightly coloured, like circus clowns. They live among the stinging arms (tentacles) of the sea anemone. Clownfish swim among the stingers, where they are safe from enemies. The anemone doesn't seem to sting the clownfish.

Sea anemone

Why are whales so big?

Whales have grown to such a huge size because they live in water. The water helps to support their enormous bulk. The blue whale is the biggest animal in the ocean – and the whole planet. It is about 30 metres long and can weigh up to 150 tonnes. Every day, it eats about 4 tonnes of tiny, shrimp-like creatures called krill!

Blue whale

Can whales sing songs?

All whales make sounds, such as squeaks and moans. The humpback whale really does seem to sing. The males probably do this to attract a mate. He may repeat his song for up to 20 hours!

Humpback whale

Stick around!

Barnacles are shellfish. They attach themselves to ships, or the bodies of grey whales and other large sea animals.

Measure

The blue whale is 30 metres long. Can you measure how long you are?

Do whales grow tusks?

The narwhal has a tusk like a unicorn's. This tusk is a long, twirly tooth that comes out of the whale's head. The males use their tusks as weapons when they fight over females. The tusk can grow to 3 metres in length.

Are there crocodiles in the sea?

Most crocodiles live in rivers and swamps. The saltwater crocodile also swims out to sea – it doesn't seem to mind the salty water. These crocodiles are huge, and can grow to be 7 metres long and one tonne in weight.

Saltwater crocodile

Find out

Turtles only come ashore for one reason. Can you find out why?

Which lizard loves to swim?

Most lizards live on land, where it is easier to warm up their cold-blooded bodies. Marine iguanas depend on the sea for food. They dive underwater to eat seaweed growing on rocks. When they are not diving, they sit on rocks and soak up the sunshine.

How deep can a turtle dive?

Leatherback turtles can dive up to 1200 metres for their dinner. They are the biggest sea turtles and they make the deepest dives. Leatherbacks feed mostly on jellyfish but also eat crabs, lobsters and starfish.

Leatherback turtle

Slithery snakes!

There are poisonous snakes in the sea. The banded sea snake and the yellow-bellied sea snake both use poison to kill their prey. Their poison is far stronger than that of land snakes.

Can seabirds sleep as they fly?

Wandering albatrosses are the biggest seabirds and spend months at sea. They are such good gliders that they even sleep as they fly. To feed, they sit on the surface of the water, where they catch creatures such as squid. An albatross has a wingspan of around 3 metres – about the length of a family car!

Wandering albatross

Think

Sea birds have webbed feet. Why do you think this is? Do you have webbed feet?

Do seabirds dig burrows?

Most seabirds make nests on cliffs.
The puffin digs a burrow on the clifftop, like a
rabbit. Sometimes, a puffin even takes
over an empty rabbit hole. Here it lays
its egg. Both parents look after the
chick when it hatches.

Puffins

Dancing birds!

Boobies are a type of seabird that live in large groups. The males have bright red or blue feet. When they are looking for a mate, they dance in front of the female, trying to attract her with their colourful feet!

Which bird dives for its dinner?

The gannet dives headfirst into the ocean to catch fish in its beak. It dives at high-speed and hits the water hard. Luckily, the gannet is protected by cushions of air inside its head that absorb most of the shock.

How do polar bears learn to swim?

Polar bears are good swimmers and they live around the freezing Arctic Ocean. They learn to swim when they are cubs, by following their mother into the water. With their big front paws, the bears paddle through the water. They can swim for many hours.

Polar bears

Imagine
Pretend to be a penguin. Imagine what life is like at the South Pole.

Are penguins fast swimmers?

Penguins are birds – but they cannot fly. All penguins are fast swimmers. The fastest swimmer is the gentoo penguin. It can reach speeds of 27 kilometres an hour underwater.

Gentoo penguin

Small and tall!

The smallest penguin is the fairy penguin at just 40 centimetres tall. The biggest is the emperor penguin at 1.3 metres in height – as tall as a seven-year-old child!

Which penguin dad likes to babysit?

Emperor penguin dads look after the baby chicks. The female lays an egg and leaves her mate to keep it warm. The penguin dad balances the egg on his feet to keep it off the freezing ice. He goes without food until the chick hatches. When it does, the mother returns and both parents look after it.

Is seaweed good to eat?

Seaweed can be very good to eat. In shallow, warm seawater, people can grow their own seaweed. It is then dried in the sun, which helps to keep it fresh. Seaweed is even used to make ice cream!

Growing seaweed

List

Make a list of the things you can eat that come from the ocean. Which of these things have you eaten before?

How do we get salt from the sea?

Sea water is salty. Salt is an important substance. In hot, low-lying areas, people build walls to hold shallow pools of sea water. The water dries up in the sun, leaving behind crystals of salt.

How are lobsters caught?

Lobsters are large shellfish that are good to eat. Fishermen catch them in wooden cages called pots. The lobsters are attracted to dead fish placed in the pots. They push the door of the pot open to get to the fish, but once inside, the lobster can't get out again.

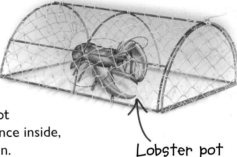

Lobster pot

Do pearls grow at sea?

Yes they do. Pearls grow inside oysters, a kind of shellfish. If a grain of sand gets stuck in an oyster's shell, it irritates its soft body. The oyster coats the grain with a substance that it uses to line the inside of its shell. In time, more coats are added and a pearl begins to form.

Are there chimneys under the sea?

Rocky chimneys on the ocean floor give off clouds of hot water. These chimneys lie deep beneath the ocean. The hot water feeds strange creatures such as tube worms and sea spiders.

Rat tail fish

Watery village!

In 1963, diver Jacques Cousteau built a village on the bed of the Red Sea. Along with four other divers, he lived there for a whole month.

Giant clams

Do monsters live in the sea?

Sea monsters do not exist. Long ago, people thought they did. The giant squid may have been mistaken for a monster. It has long arms called tentacles, and eyes as big as dinner plates.

Giant squid

What is a mermaid?

Mermaids are strange creatures with the body of a woman and a long fishy tail — but they aren't real. People once thought they lived in the sea and confused sailors with their beautiful singing.

Chimney

Sea spider

Tube worms

Write
Can you think of any stories or films about mermaids? See if you can write your own underwater mermaid story.

How long is the seashore?

Around the world there are thousands of kilometres of seashore. It can be sandy, pebbly, muddy, or rocky with high cliffs. Many interesting plants and animals make their homes on or near the shore – and so do millions of people.

Sandy seashore

which shores are the coldest?

The coldest seashores are around the North and South poles, the chilliest ends of the Earth. It is so cold here that the sea often freezes. Polar bears, penguins and seals are good at surviving on these icy shores.

Crabeater seal

Find out

Do you live by the sea? If not, look on a map to find your nearest seashore.

Trees in the breeze

Seashores can be blasted by winds from the sea that constantly blow in the same direction. These winds can make trees grow over to one side.

why do seashores have tides?

Because the Earth is spinning! As Earth spins, the Moon pulls on the sea, and the surface rises. Water flows up the shore, making a high tide. Then it flows out again, creating a low tide. Each seashore has two high tides a day.

why do seashells cling to rocks?

They cling to rocks so they don't get washed away by the tide. Animals such as limpets, mussels and barnacles live inside seashells. At high tide they open their shells to find food. At low tide, the shells shut tight so they don't dry out.

Limpet

Barnacles

Mussels

write

When you next visit a sandy beach, try writing your name in the sand with a stick.

what are seashore zones?

The area between high and low tide is called the intertidal zone. Low tide zone is wettest, and has lots of seaweed. High tide zone is drier, and has more land plants.

Fun at the beach

Sandy beaches make a great place for sports, such as horseriding, kite-flying, football and volleyball.

How big are the biggest waves?

Winds make waves, which break onto the seashore. Some waves can be 30 metres high — taller than a tower of 18 people. The biggest waves are tsunamis, caused by earthquakes shaking the sea. The tallest ever was 500 metres high!

what is a coral reef?

A coral reef is like a giant seashell. Tiny animals called coral polyps build up layers of hard, colourful coral over many years, to use as a home. It also makes a good home for other sea creatures, such as fish, rays, octopuses, turtles and crabs.

Coral reef

why do crabs walk sideways?

If crabs want to move quickly, walking sideways is best! Their flat, wide bodies help them slip into narrow hiding places. This means that their legs only bend sideways. Crabs can walk forwards, but only very slowly.

Sharks in the shallows

Some sharks, like the black-tip reef shark, are often found swimming around coral reefs in search of a snack.

Do all crabs have shells?

Most crabs have a hard shell, but hermit crabs don't. They need to find some kind of 'shell' to protect their soft bodies. Usually, they use another sea creature's old empty shell.

Christmas Island red crab

Make

Make a hermit crab from modelling clay, and give it a home made of a shell, cup or plastic lid.

Why do birds love the seaside?

Great black-backed gull

Lesser black-backed gull

Herring gull

Rock dove

Chough

Guillemot

Razorbill

Puffin

Many kinds of seabird live on and near the seashore. It's a good place to find food and raise their chicks. Seabirds make their nests on the shore or on rocky cliff ledges. They fly out over the water to catch fish.

Do beetles head for the beach?

The tiger beetle does! This shiny, green beetle lays its eggs in warm, sandy places. These beetles are often found in sand dunes – small, grassy hills of sand at the top of a beach.

Tiger beetle

Paint
Copy the picture on this page and paint a tiger beetle. Add green glitter for its shiny body.

Swimming cats
Some tigers live in mangrove forests near the coast. They like to splash in the water to cool down.

How does being sick help a chick?

Fulmars are seabirds. When they go fishing, they leave their chicks alone in their nests. If hunting animals come near the nests, the chicks squirt stinky, fishy, oily vomit to scare them away!

Does the seashore have shapes?

Sea stacks   Arch

Yes, seashores have lots of shapes. There are bays, spits, cliffs, archways and towers. They form over many years, as wind and waves batter the coast. Softer rocks get carved away into bays and hollows. Harder rocks last longer, and form sticking-out headlands.

Shingle spit

Shingle beach

Make

At a pebbly beach, make a sculpture by balancing small pebbles on top of each other in a tower.

Bay

why are pebbles round?

The pebbles on beaches are stones that have been rolled and tumbled around by waves. As they knock together, they lose their sharp corners and edges, and slowly become smooth and round.

Cave

Cliffs

what is sand made of?

Sand is made of tiny pieces of rocks and shells. Larger lumps gradually break down into grains, as the waves crash onto them and make them swirl around.

Delta

Plastic sand

On some beaches, one in every ten sand grains is actually made of plastic. It comes from litter dropped on beaches or thrown from boats.

Sandy beach

why is a curlew's beak so long?

To find its food buried in the mud, a curlew needs a long, thin beak! It sticks its beak deep into the mud to pick out worms, crabs and insects. A curlew also has long legs to wade in the water.

Curlew

measure

With a long ruler, mark out one square metre. Try to imagine thousands of seashells living in this area!

Are seashells different shapes?

Yes, they are. A seashell's shape depends on the creature that lives in it, and how it feeds and moves. Spireshells and tower shells are spirals. Clams and cockles have two hinged shells. They open them to feed, or close them to keep safe.

Clam

Tower shell

Common cockle

Laver spireshell

Painted top shell

How do penguins get out of the water?

Penguins can't fly, but they can swim fast underwater, using their wings as flippers. When they want to get out of the sea, they zoom up to the surface and shoot out of the water, landing on the ice.

Crowds of creatures

Some muddy beaches have more then 50,000 tiny shellfish living in each square metre of mud.

where might you see a bear by the sea?

You might see a bear at an estuary, the place where a river meets the sea. In parts of Canada and the United States, grizzly bears try to catch salmon as they leave the sea and head up rivers to breed. They may also nibble berries and sea plants.

Grizzly bear

what is sea pink?

Sea pink is a seashore flower. Not many plants can survive near the sea because it's so windy and salty. But sea pink is tough. It also has special parts that carry salt out of the plant through its leaves.

Sea pink

Down in one

Penguins swallow fish whole, and the fish dissolve inside their stomachs. They can bring the mush back up to feed their chicks.

why does glass come from the seashore?

Make

Make baby penguin food. Mash tinned tuna with a teaspoon of olive oil. Eat it in a sandwich!

Because it's made from sand! Glass is made by heating sand until it melts and turns clear. Long ago, people burnt sea plants such as glasswort to get chemicals for glass-making.

What hides in the sand?

Worms, shrimps, razorshells and some crabs all burrow down into the sand to hide. At high tide they come out and feed. At low tide, being under the sand helps them to stay damp, and avoid being eaten.

Gull

Shrimps

Worms

HUNT
Go on a beach treasure hunt. Look for different shells, different-coloured pebbles and seaweed.

Razorshell

42

where is the highest tide in the world?

At the Bay of Fundy in Canada, high tide is super-high! The sea level rises to around 17 metres higher than at low tide. At most beaches, the water is just 2 to 3 metres deeper at high tide.

Treasure-hunting

People love beachcombing too. It's fun to look for interesting creatures, pebbles, shells, or bits of glass that have been rubbed smooth by the sea.

Otter

Lizard

Toad

which animals go beachcombing?

A line of seaweed, driftwood, shells and litter usually collects at the 'strandline' – the level the high tide flows up to. Seabirds, and other animals such as foxes and otters, go 'beachcombing' along the strandline to look for washed-up crabs and fish to eat.

Crab

when can you see a rock pool?

When the tide goes out you might see a rock pool. Seawater gets trapped in hollows in rocks or sand. The best places to find rock pools are rocky beaches. Sea creatures shelter here at low tide.

Find out
Find a photo of a sea anemone and a photo of an anemone flower. Do they look alike?

Are there fleas at the beach?

No, there aren't any fleas, but there are little creatures that look like them. Sand hoppers stay buried in the sand all day, then come out at night to look for food.

Sand hopper

What lives in a rock pool?

All kinds of creatures live in a rock pool. These can include crabs, sea anemones, sea urchins, shrimps, shellfish, starfish, sponges, small fish and even octopuses. There are also seaweeds, which animals can hide under.

Rock pool

Super sponges
Rock pool sponges are actually simple animals! The natural sponge that you might use in the bath is a long-dead, dried-out sponge!

45

which forest grows in the sea?

Mangroves are trees that grow in salty water or seaside mud. Some seashores, especially in hot, tropical places, have mangrove forests growing along them. The mangroves' roots stick out of the ground, and get covered by the tide when it comes in.

Mangroves

why do crabs turn the ground bright red?

When red crabs march, they turn the ground into a red, moving mass! These crabs live on Christmas Island in the Indian Ocean. Twice a year, thousands of red crabs head to the sea to lay eggs. Then they go back to their forest homes.

Play
Have a crab race with your friends. You're only allowed to run sideways, like a crab!

Red crabs

Fishy cat

In South East Asia there is a wild cat that goes fishing. The fishing cat is a good swimmer, and hunts for fish and other small animals in mangrove swamps.

what is a sea cow?

Sea cows aren't really cows. They are dugongs and manatees — huge, sausage-shaped sea creatures, a bit like seals. Like a real cow, sea cows graze on plants, such as sea grass and mangrove leaves.

47

where do turtles lay their eggs?

Sea turtles live in the sea, but lay their eggs on land. Female turtles crawl up sandy beaches at night, and dig holes with their flippers, in which they lay their eggs. Then they cover them over with sand, and leave them to hatch.

← Turtle

why do baby turtles race to the sea?

When turtle eggs hatch, baby turtles climb out of their sandy nest and head for the sea. They must reach the water quickly, before they get gobbled up by a seabird, crab or fox.

Salty nose

The marine iguana is a lizard that swims in the sea to eat seaweed. Salt from the sea makes a white patch on its nose.

Find out

There are different types of turtle. Look in books or on the Internet to find out what they are.

which seabird has a colourful beak?

Puffins have bright beaks striped with orange, yellow and black. In spring, their beaks and feet become brighter, to help them find a mate. Males and females rub their beaks together to show they like each other.

Puffins

what is a coral reef?

Coral reefs are living structures that grow in the sea. They are built by millions of tiny animals, called coral polyps. When they die, new polyps grow on top. This builds up layers of coral rock over time. Some reefs, such as the Great Barrier Reef, are enormous and can be seen from the air.

Great Barrier Reef

Coral

Do trees grow underwater?

Trees do not grow underwater, but soft tree corals look like trees because they have branches. Coral reefs are sometimes called 'rainforests of the sea'. Like rainforests on land, coral reefs are important homes for millions of marine animals.

Soft tree coral

Big brains!

Octopuses are super smart animals that live near reefs. They are experts at finding prey hiding in rocky crevices.

Colour!

Choose your favourite fish from this book. Copy it onto paper and colour it in.

How do coral polyps feed?

Coral polyps live in hard, stony cups and feed on tiny animals that drift by in the water. They catch food with tiny stingers on their tentacles, as do jellyfish, which are in the same animal family as coral polyps.

can turtles swim far?

Turtles go on very long journeys across the sea to feed, mate or lay their eggs. Female turtles always return to the same beach to lay their eggs. How they find their way is still a mystery, but they don't seem to get lost!

Discover

Use an atlas to find out which country beginning with 'A' is near the Great Barrier Reef.

Turtles from *Finding Nemo*

when does a fish look like a stone?

When it is a stonefish! Stonefish are almost impossible to see when they are lying flat and still on the seabed. Their colours blend in with the rocky and sandy surfaces.

Stonefish

Show-offs!

Cuttlefish can change colour! In just a few seconds, a cuttlefish can flash colours of red, yellow, brown or black.

Do seahorses gallop?

Seahorses are fish, not horses, so they cannot run or gallop! They are not very good swimmers so they wrap their tails around seaweed to stop ocean currents carrying them away.

why are fish like lions?

Lionfish

Some fish are like lions because they hunt for food at night. Lionfish hide among rocks in the day. As the sun sets, they come out to hunt for small animals to eat. They have amazing stripes and spines on their bodies. Their spines hold venom, which can cause very painful stings.

Dive but stay alive!
Divers can use cages to watch sharks safely. The divers wear masks and carry tanks that have air inside them so they can breathe underwater.

when do birds visit reefs?

Birds visit coral reef islands to build their nests. When
their eggs hatch, the birds find plenty of fish at the reef
to feed to their chicks. Albatrosses are large sea birds,
so their chicks need lots of fish!

can slugs be pretty?

Yes they can! Like many coral
reef animals, sea slugs have amazing
colours and patterns. These warn other
animals that they are harmful to eat. Most
sea slugs are small, but
some can grow to
30 centimetres
in length.

Sea slugs

55

what lives on a reef?

A huge number of different animals live on or around reefs. They are home to fish of all shapes and sizes, including sharks. There are many other animals too — octopus, squid, slugs, sponges, starfish and urchins all live on reefs.

Black sea urchin

Sea turtle

Starfish

Do turtles lay eggs?

Yes, they do. Turtles spend most of their lives at sea, but lay their eggs on land. A female turtle digs a hole in the sand, and lays her round eggs inside it. When the eggs hatch, the baby turtles crawl back to the sea.

A sting in the tail!

Blue-spotted rays live in coral reefs and feed on shellfish, crabs and worms. They have stinging spines on their tails.

Measure

Every year coral reefs grow about 10 centimetres. How much have you grown in a year?

What do coral reefs need to grow?

The polyps that build up coral reefs need plenty of sunlight and clean water to grow. They mostly live in shallow water near land where sunlight can reach them.

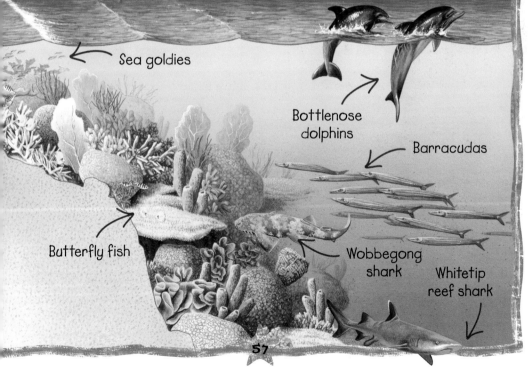

Sea goldies

Bottlenose dolphins

Barracudas

Butterfly fish

Wobbegong shark

Whitetip reef shark

Why does an octopus have eight arms?

Having eight arms allows an octopus to move quickly and grab food to eat. Each arm has suction cups that can grip onto things. An octopus grabs food with its eight strong arms, and pulls it towards its mouth.

Make
Draw lots of pictures of coral reef animals and stick them on a large piece of card to make a poster.

Blue-ringed octopus

who looks after a seahorse's eggs?

Females lay the eggs, but the males look after them in a special pouch on the front of their bodies. This keeps the eggs safe from bigger fish that might eat them. When the eggs hatch, the babies swim out of the pouch.

Don't eat me!

Little coral polyps live next to each other, but they do not always get on. Sometimes one polyp might eat its neighbour!

Do christmas trees grow on reefs?

Christmas trees do not grow on reefs – but Christmas tree worms do! These little animals live in burrows inside the reef. The feathery, spiral parts we can see are called feeding tentacles.

Christmas tree worm —

where do clownfish live?

Clownfish live in the tentacles of coral reef creatures called sea anemones. Like coral polyps, these strange-looking animals sting their prey. Clownfish have a slimy skin covering that protects them from the sting and allows them to live there unharmed.

Sea anemone

Hide

Invite some friends to join you in a game of hide and seek. Where could you hide?

Clownfish

Can seashells be deadly?

The coneshell can be! The shell is just the animal's hard outer casing — it is the soft-bodied creature inside that is the dangerous part. Coneshells hunt other animals and attack by jabbing them with a deadly venom.

Coneshell

Which shrimp likes to punch its prey?

Mantis shrimps may be small, but they can pack a big punch. They live in reefs near Australia and in the Pacific Ocean. They punch their prey to stun them, and then tuck in for a tasty meal.

can starfish be blue?

Most starfish are red or brown, but big blue ones live on some reefs. Starfish have small, tube-like feet on the undersides of their arms, which allow them to crawl over the reef. They have tiny eyes at the end of each arm, which can only see light or dark.

Starfish

Make

Make a map that shows where pirate treasure is buried on a coral island.

Do jellyfish wobble?

No, jellyfish may look like jelly, but they are living animals. They have long, stinging tentacles that hang below their bodies as they swim. Some jellyfish live around coral reefs, where there are plenty of fish to eat.

Box jellyfish

Fish hotspot!

There are more than 24,000 different types of fish in the world. Many of those live in or around coral reefs.

why did pirates bury treasure on coral islands?

Pirates are believed to have buried stolen treasure so no one could find it. There are lots of stories about pirates who buried gold and precious stones on coral islands, but we don't know how true these tales are.

Why are corals different shapes?

The shape a coral grows into depends on the type of polyp it has. Where the coral grows on the reef is also important. Brain coral grows slowly and in calm water. Staghorn and elkhorn corals grow more quickly, and in shallow water.

Brain coral

Elkhorn coral

Staghorn coral

Are there butterflies in the sea?

There is a type of butterfly living in the sea – but it isn't an insect, it's a fish! Many butterfly fish have colourful spots and stripes to help make them hard to spot.

Butterfly fish

LOOK

Find out if you can see colours better in the dark or in the light.

Going for a spin!

Dolphins visit coral reefs to feast on fish. They jump out of the water and can even spin, though no one knows why they do it!

Can fish see in the dark?

Many of animals can see in the dark! Lots of coral animals sleep during the day, but when the Sun goes down they come out to look for food or mates. Many of them, such as the red soldierfish, are much better at seeing in the dark than people are.

which crab moves house?

Hermit crabs live inside borrowed shells and move house if they find a bigger, better one. They don't have their own shells so they have to find one to protect their soft bodies. Most hermit crabs choose snail shells to live in.

Hermit crab →

Why is some coral white?

Damaged coral

Most coral is very colourful, until it dies and turns white or grey. There are many reasons why corals are dying. Dirty water is one of the most important reasons. Water that is too warm is also bad for polyps.

Slow-grow!
Giant clams can grow to be enormous – up to 150 centimetres long! They can live for 70 years.

Who looks after coral reefs?

Special ocean parks are set up to look after the animals that live on coral reefs. People are not allowed to catch the fish or damage the reef inside these protected areas.

Measure
Use a measuring tape to find out how long a giant clam is.

How do fish clean their teeth?

They get other fish to do it for them! Little fish, called wrasses, eat the bits of food stuck in the teeth of other fish, such as moray eels. The wrasses get a tasty meal and the moray eels get their teeth cleaned!

Moray eel

Are all sharks dangerous?

No, most sharks would never attack a person. Whale sharks are huge but they don't eat big animals. They swim through the water with their large mouths open. They suck in water and any little creatures swimming in it.

Whale shark

which crab wears boxing gloves?

Boxer crabs hold sea anemones in their claws, like boxing gloves. They wave them at any animals that come too close — the sight of the stinging tentacles warns other animals to stay away.

school's out!

A group of fish is called a shoal, or a school. Fish often swim in shoals because it helps them stay safe from bigger fish that might eat them.

Wrasse

Brush

We don't have wrasses, so when you brush your teeth try hard to remove every tiny bit of food.

which fish is spiky?

Pufferfish are strange-looking, poisonous fish with sharp spines. When they feel scared, pufferfish blow up their bodies to make their spines stand on end. This makes them bigger and much harder to swallow.

Pufferfish with spines relaxed

Pufferfish with spines on end

March

Imagine you are a lobster on a long march. How far can you march before you get tired?

why do lobsters march?

Coral reef spiny lobsters march to deep, dark water where they lay their eggs. They march through the night at the end of the summer. Thousands of lobsters join the march to reach a safe place to breed.

Crown-of-thorns starfish

clean teeth!

When fish such as sweetlips want their teeth cleaned, they swim to find wrasse fish and open their mouths.

How do starfish eat their prey?

Starfish turn their mouths inside out to eat. The crown-of-thorns starfish kills coral by eating the soft polyps inside. Each of these large starfish can have up to 21 arms.

What is a shark?

Blue shark

Whale shark

A shark is a meat-eating fish that lives in the sea. All sharks have a strong sense of smell to help them find their prey — the animals they hunt for food. Most sharks have a big mouth and sharp teeth.

Shark submarines!

Most submarines can't dive over 500 metres, but the Portuguese shark can dive down to over 3500 metres.

Where in the world do sharks live?

Sharks live in seas and oceans around the world. They are often found by the coast, a few kilometres from the beach. Each type of shark has its own favourite place to live.

Great white shark

Starry smooth-
hound shark

Basking shark

Sandbar shark

How many types of shark are there?

There are around 330 kinds of shark. The most common is the blue shark. Each type of shark is different in size, colour and markings. Types of shark can also behave differently.

Draw
Sketch a scary shark with big teeth chasing small fish in the sea.

73

How does a shark swim?

Sand tiger shark

A shark swims by using its fins. The tail itself is a fin, and moves from side to side using strong muscles to push the shark through the water. The fin on the top of the body is called the dorsal fin. This keeps the shark upright in the water.

Shark cookies!

The cookie-cutter shark was given its name because of how it feeds. It bites its prey and then swivels its sharp teeth in a circle to cut away a cookie-shaped lump of flesh.

How does a shark breathe?

A shark breathes through its gills, which are slits on the sides of its head. Most sharks have to keep swimming all the time so that water is always flowing over their gills, allowing them to breathe.

Dorsal fin

Gills

Play

Sharks have good night-time eyesight. When you next go to bed, see how well you can see in the dark.

Do sharks have good senses?

Yes! Sharks can see well even at night, and can smell blood from several kilometres away. Hearing is not their best sense, but they can still hear scuba divers breathing. Their ears are tiny holes just behind their eyes.

Why do sharks have pointy teeth?

So they can saw lumps of flesh off the animals they catch! The teeth are narrow with sharp areas along their edges. The great white shark's teeth grow up to 6 centimetres in length – that's about the size of your middle finger.

Do sharks go to sleep?

Most sharks don't sleep. However, whale sharks sometimes stop swimming to rest on the seabed. They can stay still like this for months. This helps them save energy when there is not much food.

Sneaky shark!

The blind shark of Australia isn't blind at all! It has thick eyelids that when shut, make the shark look blind.

Tiger shark

What do sharks eat?

Sharks eat all kinds of meat, including fish and seals. Some sharks hunt and chase their prey, or feast on dying or dead animals. Other sharks lie in wait for food, and some swim open-mouthed to swallow small prey in the water.

Great white shark

Count

Whale sharks can stay still in the water for months. Time how long you can stay still for.

Do sharks lay eggs?

Some sharks do lay eggs, but others give birth to live babies. A shark egg contains the young shark and a yolk. The yolk feeds the shark until it hatches. An empty egg case is called a 'mermaid's purse'.

50 days

100 days

Egg

Think

Sharks are not the only animals that lay eggs. How many egg-laying animals can you think of?

Do sharks look after their babies?

No they don't. As soon as they are born, baby sharks have to look after themselves. They have to hunt for their own food and protect themselves against other creatures that try to eat them.

Hungry pups!

As the young of the sand tiger shark grow inside their mother, the biggest one with the most developed teeth may feed on the smaller, weaker ones.

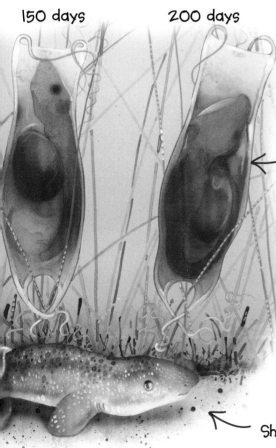

150 days

200 days

Pup developing in an egg

What are baby sharks called?

Baby sharks are called pups. They normally look like smaller versions of their parents, but have brighter colours and markings. Many pups get eaten, as they are easy prey for dolphins, sea lions and other sharks.

Shark pup

250 days

Which shark can disappear?

An angel shark can. Its wide, flat body is sand-coloured so it blends perfectly with the seabed. These sharks are called angel sharks because their fins spread out wide like an angel's wings. They can lie in wait for over a week until the right food comes along.

Angel shark

Hide

See if you can blend into your surroundings like an angel shark. Can anyone find you?

How do sharks find mates?

They use their sense of smell! When it's time to make babies, sharks give off special smells into the water to attract one another. Some sharks don't mate very often, and can become rare.

White-tip reef sharks

Do sharks have cousins?

Yes, they do – in a way. Sharks have close relations such as skates and rays. The bodies of these fish are similar to those of sharks. Stingrays have sharp spines on their tails. These contain poison that they stab into prey, or any creatures that try to attack them.

Greedy shark!

A dead greenland shark was once found with a whole reindeer in its stomach! These sharks usually eat fish and squid, but they have been known to eat dead whales.

Which fish stick to sharks?

Fish called sharksuckers do! Using a ridged sucker on their heads, they stick onto large sharks so they don't have to swim, and can go wherever the shark goes. When the shark finds a meal, the sharksucker can break off and steal what food is left.

Bull shark

Sharksucker

White-tip reef shark

Cleaner wrasse

Do sharks have friends?

Sharks and cleaner wrasse fish help each other. Sharks even let these fish into their mouths without eating them. The cleaner wrasse eat the dirt on the shark's teeth, and in return the shark gets its teeth cleaned.

Glowing sharks!

Lanternsharks can glow in the dark. The light they create attracts small creatures such as fish and squid, so the shark can snap them up.

Do sharks lose their teeth?

Yes – most shark's teeth are quite narrow and can snap off. New teeth are always growing to replace any that are lost. Some sharks lose over 3000 teeth in their lifetime.

Which shark is as big as a whale?

The whale shark is. In fact it is the biggest shark of all. It can grow to be as long as five cars – that's 18 metres in length. Whale sharks can weigh more than 12 tonnes – that's the same weight as 12 large horses.

Whale shark

Saw shark

Which shark digs for its dinner?

The saw shark does! Its long nose is surrounded by teeth, so it looks like a saw. They use their noses to dig up prey from the seabed. Then they slash and tear at the food.

Dinner time!

Krill look like small shrimps and are up to 3 centimetres in length. Whale sharks feed by taking water into their mouths and trapping krill before swallowing them.

Find out

Use the Internet or books to find information and pictures about krill. Where do they live?

Why are sharks so scary?

Sharks seem scary because they are so big and have sharp teeth. We feel unable to protect ourselves against them. Sharks are often shown in films and on television as more dangerous than they really are.

Which shark wears a disguise?

The wobbegong shark seems to. However, its lumpy body, with patterns and bumps, is what actually makes it look just like rocks and seaweed. It also has a wide, flat body to help it hide on the seabed. A wobbegong will wait for fish to swim past and then gobble them up.

Wobbegong shark

Shark enemies!

Even sharks have enemies. Large, powerful sharks such as hammerheads are attacked by elephant seals, which can weigh up to 5 tonnes.

What is the fastest shark?

The mako shark is. It can swim at more than 55 kilometres an hour. It is speedy because of its slim shape. The mako can also jump well, leaping up to 10 metres out of the water.

Mako shark

Which shark will eat anything?

Tiger sharks are the least fussy eaters. They have been known to eat all kinds of strange things — bottles, tools, car tyres, and in one case, even a type of drum called a tom-tom!

Remember

From what you have read, can you remember which sharks like to live on the seabed?

Can small sharks be fierce?

They can when they hunt in a group. Pygmy sharks are one of the smallest types of shark, at only 18 to 20 centimetres in length. By working together they can attack and kill fish much larger than themselves. Luckily, pygmy sharks are harmless to humans.

Pygmy sharks

Think

If you had discovered the megamouth shark what would you have called it? What other shark names can you think of?

Do sharks use hammers?

A hammerhead does! Its hammer-shaped head gives it a better sense of smell. This is because its nostrils are far apart, one on each side of its head. This helps the hammerhead to find out quickly where a smell is coming from, so it can track down its food.

Megamouth shark

Tiny sharks!

The smallest sharks could lie curled up in your hand. The dwarf lanternshark is just 20 centimetres in length.

Which shark is a big-mouth?

The megamouth shark's mouth is more than 1.3 metres in width. Inside are rows of tiny teeth. This shark swims through shoals of fish with its mouth wide open, trapping and swallowing its prey.

Can sharks be prickly?

Yes they can! Most sharks have tough, slightly spiky skin. The bramble shark is a deep-water shark that has very prickly skin. It is covered in large, sharp thorn-like spikes that act as protection from predators.

Bramble shark

Hot sharks!

Unlike most sharks, great whites are partly warm-blooded. This helps the muscles in their bodies work better, allowing them to swim quickly when hunting.

When is a shark like a zebra?

When it is young, a zebra shark is covered in stripes. It has dark and pale stripes that run along its body. As it gets older it grows up to 3 metres in length, and its stripes separate, turning into spots.

Adult zebra shark

Draw

Design a poster to show why we need to look after sharks, and how people can help.

Do sharks eat people?

Sharks very rarely eat people. If they do attack, it's because they think we are prey, or because they are hungry. Most people survive shark attacks, because once sharks realize the person is not their usual food, they leave them alone.

Are all sharks dangerous?

No, most sharks are harmless. However some sharks such as the great white, tiger and bull shark have been known to attack people. These sharks are always on the look-out for food, which is why they can be dangerous.

Count

Now you have read this book, how many different kinds of shark can you remember?

A great white shark

Do people eat sharks?

Some people do. In places such as Asia, shark fin soup is very popular. People hunting sharks for food has led to some sharks becoming very rare. We need to protect sharks or they may die out forever.

Shark watching!

Some people go on trips in glass-bottomed boats to see sharks. This doesn't upset the sharks, and it allows people to understand them better.

How can we learn about sharks?

Scientists can learn about sharks by watching them in the wild. This can be dangerous if the sharks are hungry, or come too close. To stay safe, people watch sharks from inside diving cages where they can't get hurt.

Index